SCHIRMER'S LIBRARY
OF MUSICAL CLASSICS

JOHANN SEBASTIAN BACH

Two- and Three-Part Inventions

For the Piano

Edited by

CZERNY, GRIEPENKERL and ROITZSCH

IN TWO BOOKS

(Also in One Book Complete)

TWO-PART INVENTIONS — Library Vol. 850

THREE-PART INVENTIONS — Library Vol. 851

TWO- AND THREE-PART INVENTIONS
(Complete) — Library Vol. 813

A Second-Piano Part to the
Fifteen Two-Part Inventions
by Louis Victor Saar is published by G. Schirmer, Inc.

G. SCHIRMER, Inc.

DISTRIBUTED BY

HAL•LEONARD®
CORPORATION
7777 W. BLUEMOUND RD. P.O. BOX 13819 MILWAUKEE, WI 53213

Printed in the U.S.A. by G. Schirmer, Inc.

PREFACE

J. S. BACH appears to have written the 2-part and 3-part Inventions for his pupils expressly as a preparation for his larger works—more especially for the "Well-tempered Clavichord"—and for this purpose they cannot be too highly recommended. Even at the present day, assiduous practice of these Inventions will be of the utmost utility to each and every talented student of pianoforte-playing who wishes to rise above mediocrity, as regards developing his fingers and his musical taste. For in none of the recent, easier piano-pieces does the left-hand part contain such an independent treatment of the theme, as in these Inventions.

The title which Bach bestowed on these Inventions reads, literally:

"A faithful Guide, whereby admirers of the Clavichord are shewn a plain Method of learning not only to play clean in two Parts, but likewise in further Progress to manage three

obbligato Parts well and correctly, and at the same time not merely how to get good *Inventions* [ideas], but also how to develop the same well; but above all, to obtain a *cantabile* Style of playing, and together with this to get a strong Foretaste of [the art of] Composition."

The keys common to both sets are C-major, C-minor, D-major, D-minor, Eb-major, E-major, E-minor, F-major, F-minor, G-major, G-minor, A-major, A-minor, Bb-major, B-minor. The 2-part Inventions were composed in Cöthen; those in 3-parts, on the other hand, were probably not finished until the beginning of the Leipzig period. Of the two original manuscripts of this work, one is in the "Clavierbüchlein für W. F. Bach" (Cöthen, 1720); the other, with numerous emendations, was formerly in the possession of Ph. E. Bach, and passed later into Louis Spohr's hands.

Fifteen Two-part Inventions.

Fifteen Two-part Inventions.

Johann Sebastian Bach.

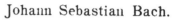

1.

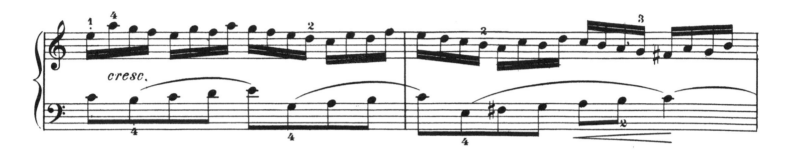

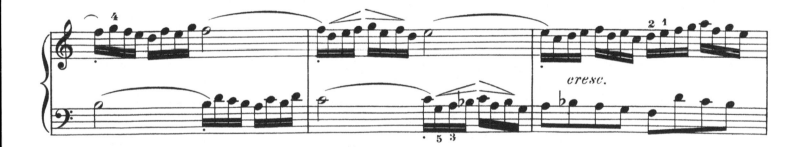

Allegro moderato. ($\quarternote$=108)

2.

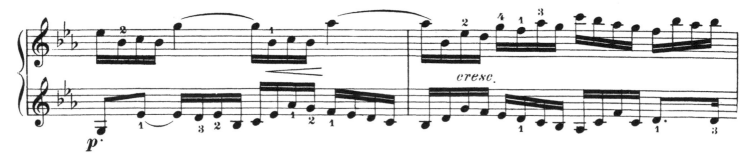

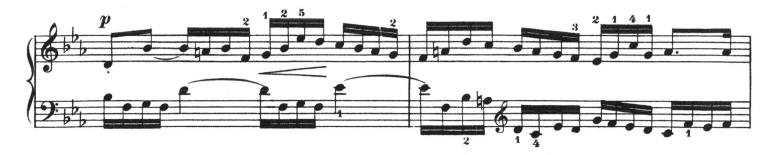

Vivace. ($\bullet$.=80)

3.

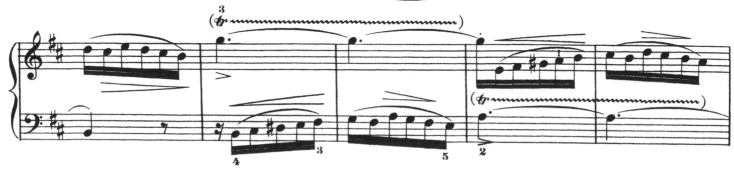

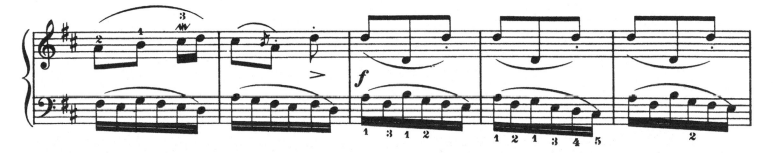

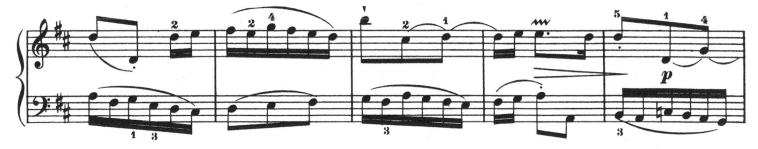

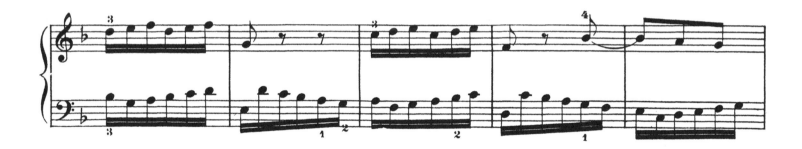

Allegro moderato. ($\quad$ = 108)

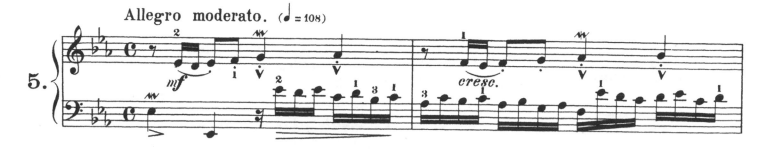

5.

Allegretto. (♪ = 144)

6.

14

7.

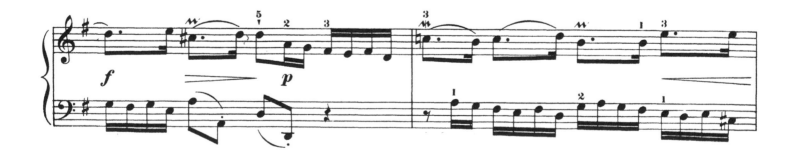

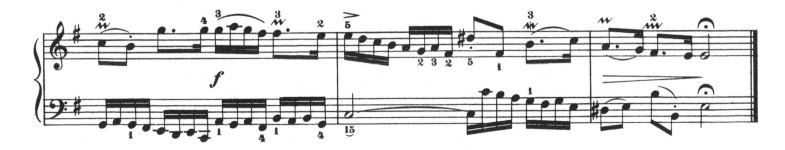

8.

9.

Con spirito. (♩=116)

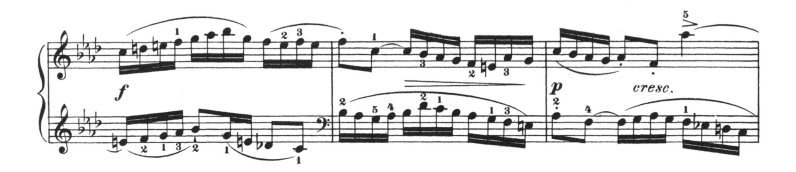

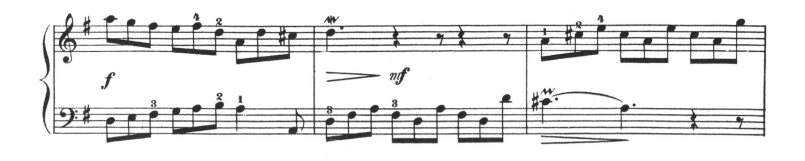

Allegro moderato. (= 108)

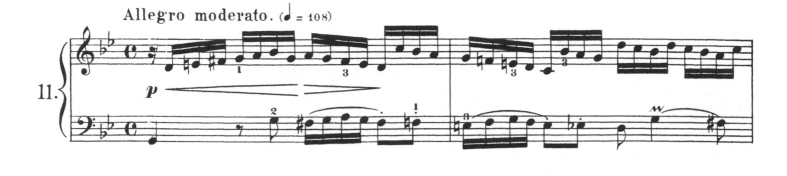

11.

Allegro giocoso. (♩. = 84)

12.

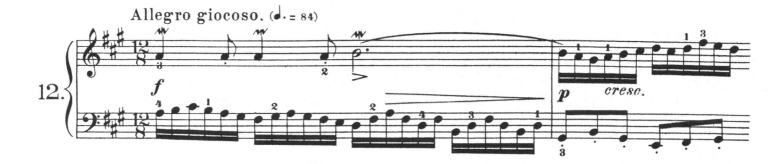

Allegro tranquillo. ($\bullet$ = 104)

13.

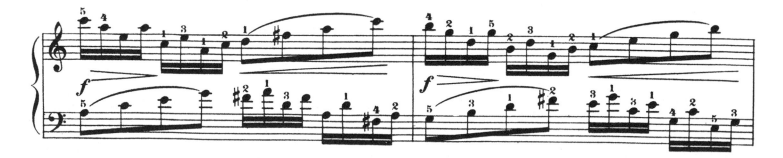

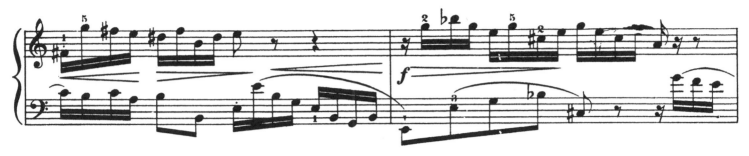

Moderato. (♩ = 88)

14.

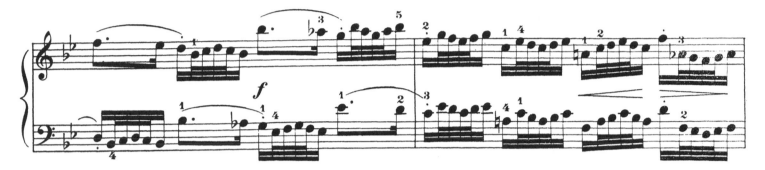

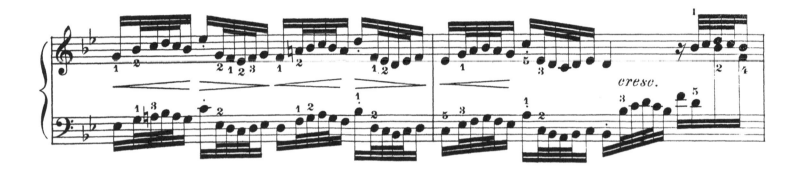

Allegro non troppo (♩ = 104)

15.